Soccer Intelligence

Soccer Training Tips To Improve Your Spatial Awareness and Intelligence In Soccer

Chest Dugger

Table Of Contents

Table Of Contents 2
Free Gift Included 4
ABOUT THE AUTHOR 5
DISCLAIMER 7
Introduction 8
First Touch Into Space 15
Drills To Develop A Good First Touch Into Space 18
Movement Without The Ball 50
Drills To Improve Movement Without The Ball 54
Choosing Between Passes 72
Drills To Improve Intelligent Passing 77
Predicting Opponent's Passing 89
Drills To Improve Passing Interception 92
Bonus – The Best Drill Of All Time 103
Conclusion 109

Free Gift Included

As part of our dedication to help you succeed in your career, we have sent you a free soccer drills worksheet. This is the "Soccer Training Work Sheet" drill sheet. This is a list of drills that you can use to improve your game; as well as a methodology to track your performance on these drills on a day-to-day basis. We want to get you to the next level.

Click on the link below to get your free drills worksheet.

https://soccertrainingabiprod.gr8.com/

You can also get this book for free as an audiobook on Audible along with a free 1-month Audible membership. Just sign up for it using the link below:

https://www.audible.com/pd/B07G24HPWN/?source_code=AUDFPWS0223189MWT-BK-ACX0-123516&ref=acx_bty_BK_ACX0_123516_rh_us

ABOUT THE AUTHOR

Chest Dugger is a pen name for our soccer coaching team, Abiprod. Abiprod is a team of passionate professional coaches and fans, based in UK and Australia. You can check us out at www.abiprod.com

We have been fans of the beautiful game for decades, coaching junior and senior teams. Like every soccer fan around the globe, we watch and play the beautiful game as much as we can. Whether we're fans of Manchester United, Real Madrid, Arsenal or LA Galaxy; we share a common love for the beautiful game.

Through our experiences, we've noticed that there's very little information for the common soccer fan who wants to escalate his game to the next level. Or get their kids started on the way. This is especially the case for those who live outside Europe and South America. Expensive soccer coaching and methodology is pretty rare in even rich countries like USA and Australia.

Being passionate about the game, we want to get the message across to as many people as possible. Through our soccer coaching blog, books and products; we aim to bring the best of soccer coaching to the world. Though we are starting off in USA and Australia, anyone who's passionate about the beautiful game can use our tactics and strategies.

DISCLAIMER

Copyright © 2018

All Rights Reserved

No part of this book can be transmitted or reproduced in any form including print, electronic, photocopying, scanning, mechanical, or recording without prior written permission from the author.

While the author has taken the utmost effort to ensure the accuracy of the written content, all readers are advised to follow information mentioned herein at their own risk. The author cannot be held responsible for any personal or commercial damage caused by information. All readers are encouraged to seek professional advice when needed.

Introduction

Consider the greatest players the beautiful game has ever seen. Pele and Puskas, Maradona – from the present time, Messi and Ronaldo. The likes of Zinedine Zidane, Thierry Henry and Dennis Bergkamp, the great readers of the game such as Beckebauer and Bobby Moore and that devastating finisher, Gerd Muller. When we try to analyze what it is that made these players so successful and held in such regard, a number of similarities come to mind.

They are, of course, mostly strikers, Beckenbauer and Moore apart. They played in the busiest, most challenging area of the pitch and in a position that could, and frequently did, change games. That is certainly true of the attacking players, but also applies to those with more defensive duties. Interestingly, though, the two defenders listed were known for their ball playing skills as much as their defensive ones.

Each possessed pace, physical strength, fast feet. Each could control a ball in an instant, were balanced in their running and hard in their shooting. But there is something more that turns the merely very

8

good into the exceptional, at whatever level they choose to play. And that is that indefinable quality we call soccer intelligence.

Intelligent people in whatever field they work know that simple works best. Soccer is, at its heart, a simple game. Pass the ball, move into space (where it is easier to control a pass and to deliver a return), move the ball on. When the chance arises, attempt to score a goal. If you are a defender, try to deny the other side space. A simple pass is easier to complete than a complex one. Intercepting the ball is easier than winning it through a tackle. Moving into space, finding a good angle and communicating well makes a pass easier to deliver for a team mate. Intelligence and simplicity might sound as though they should be opposites, but in fact they are close bed fellows.

"Simple"

The purpose of this book is to define soccer intelligence, to break it down into its constituent parts and, importantly, present drills the good coach can use with his or her team to develop that intelligence to its greatest potential.

Important

Because it is a fact that those with innate ability to read the game, anticipate passes (from both teams), to find space and utilize it contrive to make that ability of theirs better, more finely honed, even more effective than it might otherwise be.

9

So, let us start at the beginning by attempting the challenging task of defining soccer intelligence.

What Is Soccer Intelligence?

While different analysts might want to put their own interpretation on the term, few would disagree that this nebulous entity is made up of the following very tangible aspects.

Understanding of the Game – We do not become chess masters without playing, we do not get our University degree without working at the subject, similarly people with soccer intelligence have a great understanding of the game. We do not need to practice drills to achieve this, gaining understanding of the game is more fun than that (although, of course, the practices that follow in this book are entertaining in the extreme!). We gain expertise about the game by watching it, by playing it, by reading about it and by discussing it.

Imitation is the greatest form of flattery and understanding something is really just following what the best exponents achieve and trying to replicate their actions and their decisions. Bobby Moore may have had the soccer intelligence to mean that he rarely had to make a

10

one on one tackle, but he achieved this ability to read the game through following the practices of his own heroes.

Developing Spatial Awareness – In other words, knowing where our, or our players', bodies are in relationship to others around them. It is this awareness that tells players with soccer intelligence where to pass, when to play the ball first time, when to bring it under control, where to play a first touch into space, where to make runs.

Having the Skills To Apply – Of course, even the player with the greatest soccer intelligence will not become an effective team member without the necessary skills to maximize that potential. Although, of course, many would argue that this is where good coaches come in. Coaches are often players who understand the game but either never had, or no longer possess, the physical skills to make a difference on the pitch.

This book will focus on developing spatial awareness, and the skills needed to maximize that awareness on the pitch. We will look at developing first touch into space, movement without the ball, including movement into space. We will examine and practice ways to select the correct pass, and also how to predict the passes of others so that they can be intercepted.

Because these are the elements that make up soccer intelligence, and by breaking that down into these constituent parts, and practising them, we can make ourselves, or the members of our teams, more intelligent soccer players.

The Drills

Each pair of chapters in this book takes an aspect of spatial awareness leading to soccer intelligence. Firstly, it explains the importance of the facet in question to the playing the game, and then it offers a number of drills which will help players develop in that particular area.

Any of us who have coached widely know that the biggest problem with drills is getting them set up so that everybody understands what they are doing. Once the drill is understood, it can really deliver the benefits it seeks to give.

Therefore, the drills are written in a way that can be delivered verbatim, if wished, to the players. Each drill consists of a number of elements:

- A grade – easy, moderate or difficult. This grade relates to the ease with which the drill can be operated.
- A Name, so that when the drill is used again, the coach can simply say, for example, 'Set up and run through "First Touch"'
- An objective – the skill or aspect of soccer intelligence the drill seeks to develop.
- Space Required – this can be adapted to the skill level and age of the group undertaking the drill. Generally, the more space available the easier the drill becomes – space is all in soccer. Grids can be painted onto practice pitches or set up with cones. If this is difficult, the drills can be adapted to work in an already marked area, such as the penalty box, center circle or half of the pitch.
- Number of Players Involved – This is per drill. Most of these drills can be run by multiple groups at once, provided there are enough resources and space.
- Other Equipment – We keep this as simple as possible. Because the book is written by a coach, we know how hard it can be to set up drills that need complicated arrangements with multiple resources.
- Player Roles, Player Actions and Player Skills – In these three sections (where the roles are repeated, the players are put into groups) the information can simply be read or paraphrased to the players. Especially with younger, or less experienced groups, it often works best to deal with a player's (or group of players') role individually. So, by following the given instructions, each player can learn what they have

to do in the drill, what their individual contribution to the drill looks like, and what skills they will be personally developing. When players know what they are seeking to achieve, their motivation improves. When their motivation is high, they tend to be more successful in what they do.

- Organization – This section explains how the drill runs, and often includes coaching points.

- Development – many coaches will devise their own adaptations of the basic drills, but in this section are some suggestions as to how the drill can be made more challenging or adapted to work on different aspects of soccer intelligence.

Enough words let us get down to business.

First Touch Into Space

When speaking to scouts and coaches and asking them what it is that tells them that a player might one day turn into a professional, they will offer various answers. Athleticism, speed, commitment, physicality – of course, soccer intelligence.

But one characteristic stands out as the first thing a coach or scout will look for. Something that is relatively easy to spot, and which, with practice can be mastered. That is a player's first touch.

The way they shape their body on the half turn, the natural position of the arms to provide protection and balance. Even more importantly, the weighting they give to their touch on the ball. Does the foot cushion the ball as it arrives? Are they comfortable taking the ball on their instep? On the outside of their boot? Can they control a ball that is off the ground? Can the player move their feet to get into position quickly to receive the ball, thus meaning they are in the best place to exert strong control, and can concentrate on watching the ball and getting their head and arms into position, rather than lunging desperately to stop the object running away from them.

But bringing the ball just under control is not enough. Soccer is a team game requiring fluid and rapid movement of the ball. Controlling it without applying a first touch which moves the ball into space slows down the team's play. It allows defenders to get into position to mark attackers and intercept the next pass. It allows the opposition to put pressure on the player with the ball.

And when under pressure, it is far more likely that the next pass will be poor, either intercepted or putting the team mate in receipt under extra pressure. Thus, that first touch which saw the ball controlled, but in a way that did not create space might lead to a loss of possession three passes down the line.

We have all heard the commentators saying, as possession is lost and the ball heads up to the other end of the pitch: 'It got stuck under his feet.' This is the situation where the player in question has received the pass, controlled the ball dead, but in doing so removed his options of a quick pass. He has then been tackled, or has delivered a poor next ball. Or, perhaps a great pass has put a player through on goal, but the first touch has been poor and the angle for the shot has worsened, or a defender, perhaps the goalkeeper, has been able to intercept. Maybe, simply, the striker has fallen over the ball as his or her first touch saw it trapped between his rapidly moving feet.

The first touch can take many forms, and in the next chapter are a number of basic drills to practice a first touch into space in many ways.

The most common is the first touch into space to create the opportunity for a pass or, less often, a dribble. The first touch into space, however, does not have to be with the foot. It could be a chest into space, or a flicked on header, perhaps even a cushioned header for a team mate to receive.

Or, most exciting of all, a first touch which creates the opportunity for a goal scoring chance.

The drills outlined in the next chapter provide ways of developing and reinforcing the first touch of players. They can be adapted for different situations, and moulded to fit the needs of our teams.

Drills To Develop A Good First Touch Into Space

What happens on the training ground is what gets transferred onto the pitch. Therefore, since a good first touch is essential to retaining possession, and a touch into space creates pace into a move, secures control of the play and can allow for attacking possibilities, these are the skills which must be practiced during training sessions.

Drill Number One - Easy

Name of Drill: First Touch.

Objective of Drill: To develop a good first touch which can enable plays to be built upon it.

Space Required: Two lines, approximately 10 meters apart. The lines do not have to be marked.

Number of Players Involved (multiple spaces can be used for larger groups): Two.

Other Resources: 1 x ball.

Roles of Players Involved:

- *Player One* – Receiver.
- *Player Two* – Feeder.

Actions of Players Involved:

- *Player One* – Receiving the ball with a good first touch.
- *Player Two* – Feeding in passes of different accuracy and style.

Key Skills of Player Involved:

- *Player One* – The receiver should:
  o Concentrate fully on the ball, not being distracted by movement around them;

- Drop their receiving foot backwards slightly, to cushion receipt of the ball, then move it slightly in the direction they wish the ball to travel;
- Ensure that their weight is over the ball, so that it does not bobble into the air;
- Protect the ball from opponents by ensuring that their body is between the opponent and the ball.
* *Player Two* – The feeder simply presents the ball accurately to the person trying the drill.

Organisation Of Drill: This is a very simple drill. But repetition is required so that the skill is embedded. The feeder sends ten passes to the receiver, so that they can control the ball with their preferred foot. The receiver controls the ball by knocking it, under control one half of a meter in front of them.

The drill is repeated ten times and then the players swap positions.

Development: The feeder begins to vary the type of pass they send to the receiver. Passes go to the right foot, then the left foot. Some are straight, some are wider, so that the receiver has to move to get into line with the pass. A further development can be to send passes in the air, at knee height. Here, the receiver moves their body so that they can still cushion the ball and knock it the half meter in front of them, but will need to do the control with the receiving foot off of the ground. Head over the ball and arms out for balance are two key skills here.

Drill Two - Easy

Name of Drill: First Touch Into Space.

Objective of Drill: To practice controlling the ball with a first touch that moves in to the left, right or behind the receiver.

Space Required: Two lines 10 meters apart. Again, they do not have to be physical lines.

Number of Players Involved (multiple spaces can be used for larger groups): Two.

Other Resources: 1 x ball.

Roles of Players Involved:

- *Player One* – Receiver.

- *Player Two* – Feeder.

Actions of Players Involved:

- *Player One* – To receive the ball under control, knocking it into space with their first touch.
- *Player Two* – To provide accurate passing feeds to the receiver.

Key Skills Of Players Involved:

- *Player One* –

  o Controlling the ball with the inside of the foot, knocking it into space to the stronger side. In the match situation this skill is used when an opposition player is closing quickly, and the receiver wishes to draw them in before shifting the ball into space.
    - *Start with the direction of the strongest foot – i.e. right footer to the right.*
    - *Turn the opposite shoulder (i.e. left shoulder for right footer).*
    - *Drop the receiving foot back, as for a normal first touch, but move it towards the direction the ball will travel as the pass is received.*
    - *Follow the ball quickly as it moves to the required direction.*

- *Note: Rarely would the ball be controlled with the instep to move it to the other side of the receiving foot, i.e. left side for a right footer. This is because the ball naturally travel backwards and sideways in this case, making it harder to control.*
- *This is why the best players are comfortable using either foot. The options where they can put their first touch double.*

o Controlling the ball with the outside of the foot, knocking it into space both to the left and right. Although this is a slightly harder skill, it is more commonly employed. It is used when there is less pressure on the ball, or the next pass will switch the direction of play.
- *Turn the same shoulder as the foot that will play the ball (i.e. right shoulder for right footer) slightly towards the ball.*
- *Move the receiving foot forwards (rather than backwards as with an instep control), angling it so that the ball will strike the front middle of the outside of the boot.*
- *Flick the ankle in the direction the ball is to travel as the foot and the ball come into contact. Since this method of first touch is used usually when there is less pressure on the ball, the ball should be knocked one to two meters to the side.*
- *Drop the leading shoulder slightly and accelerate in the direction the ball has travelled.*

    o Controlling the ball with the inside middle of the foot, knocking it into space behind the receiver. This technique tends to be used when there is pressure coming fast onto the ball, and the main aim is to retain possession.

    ▪ *Drop the receiving foot back as though about to knock the ball forward into space.*

    ▪ *Turn the opposite shoulder slightly towards the direction from which the ball is travelling.*

    ▪ *Ensure contact is with the instep, towards the middle and back of the foot (if too far forward, the ball with cannon into the other leg, causing a probable loss of possession)*

    ▪ *If the ball is simply allowed to strike the receiving foot, it will run behind the other leg, slightly to the opposite direction of the foot (i.e. back and slightly to the left for a right footer); if more space is required with the touch, then the foot flicks the ball as it makes contact, but the ball still moves behind the receiver.*

    ▪ *The receiver turns quickly 180 degrees, ensuring the direction they turn is towards the ball, so that it remains protected (i.e. for a right footer controlling the ball backwards and slightly to the left, the receiver does their 180 degree turn to the left.)*

- *Player Two* – This player simply delivers accurate passes.

Organisation Of Drill: Again, this is a simple drill, but with regular repetition the skills being practised will become embedded in players. The feeder ensures that passes are delivered to the correct position, firstly straight to the receiver.

The receiver practises shifting the ball to the left, then the right, then behind them so that, in a match situation, they can automatically shift the ball into the direction most appropriate for the situation. Until the development stage, passes are straight, with the receiver shifting their body to allow the first touch into space to occur as required.

Again, the drill should be practised ten times then the participants swap positions.

Development: As with drill one, the feeder begins offering passes of differing accuracy and height, so that the receiver must move their body into position to control the ball in the way required.

Drill Three – Moderate

Name of Drill: Coping with Pressure On The Ball.

Objective of Drill: To play a first touch into space when under pressure from the front.

Space Required: 10 x 10 meter grid.

Number of Players Involved (multiple spaces can be used for larger groups): Three.

Other Resources: 1 x ball.

Roles of Players Involved:

- *Player One* – Receiver.
- *Player Two* – Tackler.
- *Player Three* – Feeder.

Actions of Players Involved:

- *Player One* – The receiver takes a first touch that puts the ball into space.
- *Player Two* – The tackler creates a semi pressured situation by pressing the ball, but in a way that allows the drill to be practised.

- *Player Three* – Feeds the ball with accurate passes.

Key Skills Of Players Involved:

- *Player One* – Pressure from the front:
  o The receiver uses the skills in drills in two to create space.
  o The receiver makes the decision as to the best way to maintain possession while also creating space with the first touch.
    ▪ *Safe Option* – the safest option is to take the ball into space behind. This means the tackler cannot get the ball without committing a foul; often the touch into space will be to draw the foul, allowing play to be restarted with possession. Alternatively, a simple pass back to a player in more space can follow.
    ▪ *Positive Possession Option* – This is a low risk option, will usually enable possession to be retained, but will not create the space for a really devastating follow up pass. Here, the touch into space occurs away from the direction the tackler is pressing from (i.e. if the tackler is coming from the receiver's right, they will take the pass on the outside of their left foot, moving it laterally away from the tackler.) This has the advantage of removing the risk of tackle, provided the skill is carried out correctly, but the tackler will already be heading in the direction of the ball, so will be able to make the second close down quickly and easily.

- *The receiver, with this option, should move their body between the ball and the tackler after the touch into space. Since (provided the touch is a good one) the ball will be in playing distance', this is not obstruction. It should not get penalised by the referee.*
- *Risky Option – Here the first touch takes the ball back across the direction from which the tackler is coming. The skills are as in Drill Two, but here the ball will be swept to the side with a little more force, and at 90 degrees or more from horizontal. Otherwise, the risk of interception is too great.*
- *After playing the ball, the receiver needs to rise over the oncoming tackler, to avoid injury. Either, a foul will be given, or more space created since the tackler will have to re-balance to change direction. This gives the opportunity for the receiver to play a pass with time, or embark on a dribble.*
- *Player Two* – The tackler seeks to close down the ball. As the drill develops, they can try to win possession.
- *Player Three* – The feeder delivers accurate passes into feet.

Organisation Of Drill: The feeder stands in the centre of one line of the grid. Opposite stands the receiver about one and a half meters in front of the line. (This is to give guidance for the touch into space that goes behind the receiver. If this touch crosses the line, it is too loose and in a match may well result on a second opponent nipping in to take control of the ball). The tackler stands on the same line as the feeder, but in the corner. As the ball is passed, the tackler attempts to close down the ball, and win possession.

After ten repeats, the players swap positions. Once the basic skill is mastered by a player, when they return to the receiver position, the development ideas below can be employed.

Development: The drill can be developed, and made truer to the match situation, by the tackler starting from closer to the receiver, and the feeder sending in less accurate passes, or some that are in the air (not above knee height) or bobbling.

Drill Four – Moderate

Name of Drill: First Touch Into Space With Pressure From Behind.

Objective of Drill: To maintain good possession when there is pressure from behind.

Space Required: One 10 x 10 meter grid.

Number of Players Involved (multiple spaces can be used for larger groups): Three.

Other Resources: 1 x ball.

Roles of Players Involved:

- *Player One* – Receiver.
- *Player Two* – Tackler.
- *Player Three* – Feeder.

Actions of Players Involved:

- *Player One* – Receives the ball from the front, while protecting against pressure from behind.
- *Player Two* – Pressures the ball from behind the receiver. The pressure should increase as the drill develops, until by the end genuine attempts are made to win the ball.
- *Player Three* – Feeds in passes to the receiver.

Key Skills Of Players Involved:

- *Player One* – Employs the relevant skills from drill two.

    o *The receiver's rear arm should extend backwards to make contact with the tackler.*

- *Contact should be in the chest area – higher than this could result in a foul and potentially a yellow or even red card for violent conduct.*
- *It needs to be with the flat of the hand, or fingers. The opponent's shirt cannot be held.*
- *If the player can be felt, then the first touch should be forwards, if they cannot, then there could be time to take the ball laterally with the first touch. This can only be judged by the spatial awareness of the player and the communication from team mates.*
- *As the first touch occurs, the receiver pushes off the tackler. This has a double effect. It creates forward momentum for the receiver, so that they can advance onto their first touch more quickly. It puts the weight of the tackler backwards, slowing down their next move.*
- *A further advantage is that the receiver can feel whether the tackler is going to try to come round them to intercept the ball.*
- *If this is sensed, the receiver swivels their hips to keep them between the tackler and the ball.*
- *They take the pass on their now rearmost foot.*
- *They angle the foot, inside or outside, to take the ball behind and away from the tackler.*
- *After the touch they complete the swivel of the hips, putting their whole body between tackler and ball, and move away. This is called 'turning' an opponent.*

- *They need to beware of making contact with their hips. Sometimes, tacklers will seek this, and go down if the contact is made. Referees will sometimes consider turning with contact as illegal and award a free kick against the receiver.*
- *Player Two* – The tackler should attempt to win the ball without committing a foul. If the drill is carried out correctly, this should be impossible.
- *Player Three* – Passes accurately to the feet of the receiver.

Organisation Of Drill: The feeder passes into the feet of the receiver. The tackler pressures the ball. The receiver controls the ball with a first touch that takes it away from the tackler. The drill is completed ten times, then players change positions.

Development: As with other drills in this section, this drill can be developed by the feeder offering different kinds of passing.

- Less accurate passing, which will require the receiver to move into position.
- Passing to the chest.
  o Here the receiver has three options.
    - *They can make a big chest (dropping their arms to their sides and pushing them backwards), and firmly chest the ball back in the*

direction it came with a return pass. The skill is to make the chest big, and push firmly at the ball on contact.

- They can play a sideways touch into space. Here, the chest twists on contact to direct the ball in the desired direction.
- They can push less firmly at the ball, dropping their knees to push the ball upwards and create the opportunity for a second touch.

- Passing at head height.
  o Again, there are a couple of options.
    - A header pass, either back the way the ball came, or cushioned to another player to their side.
    - A flick header into space. This involves turning and flicking the head on contact, and aiming to cushion the ball so it moves softly both upwards and in the direction desired. The player then accelerates past the tackler, who is move forwards, not sideways, into the space created.
- Off the ground passing. These can be difficult to push into space with a first touch, as the pressure from the tackler can affect balance.
  o If this is the case, the receiver should aim to put their first touch in front of them, close to their body. This is done by withdrawing the forward movement of the foot on contact with the ball.
  o Space is then created with the second touch. It is a less effective way of making space, and players should be encouraged to pass on the ground when possible.

Drill Five - Difficult

Name of Drill: First touch into space in match situation.

Objective of Drill: To replicate the work done in purely training situations into more realistic match situations.

Space Required: 9 x 10 x 10 meter grids in a 3 x 3 square. The drill can be worked on using half a pitch and allocating zones for defenders to protect.

Number of Players Involved (multiple spaces can be used for larger groups): Ten in two teams of five.

Other Resources: 6 x balls, coloured bibs (for example, four red and one orange for defensive players, four blue and one white for offensive players).

Roles of Players Involved:

- *Player One* – Feeder; player one also acts as a receiver.
- *Player Group Two* – Four more receivers.
- *Player Three* – Free Defender, or tackler.

- *Player Group Four* – Four more defenders, or tacklers.

Actions of Players Involved:

- *Player One* – This player starts each play, then joins in as an extra attacking receiver. This player may go into 10 x10 meter grid at any time.
- *Player Group Two* – The other four attackers. These players begin in a single grid square, and can move into any adjacent grid square to receive a pass.
- *Player Three* – The free defender may go into any grid square to make a tackle.
- *Player Group Four* – These remaining defenders begin in a 10 x 10 meter grid square and must remain within it.

Key Skills Of Players Involved: This is a fast moving drill, where skills are practised in a real time situation. The football skills are as developed in Drills 1-4, but here intelligence of movement and positioning is developed. Communication is another skill, and the coach should encourage both teams to do so.

- *Player One* – This player will always be a spare, able to make the decision to move into a square that is undefended to receive an easy pass and get the attacking team into a position to move forward once more. The skill is to judge when to demand the easy pass, which can be controlled under no pressure to restart the attack.

- *Player Group Two* – Additional skills to those in Drills 1-4 practised here are communication and decision making after the first touch.
- *Player Three* – Communication. This is the defensive player with the most flexibility of movement and so the one who should take on the organisational duties of the defence.
- *Player Group Four* – Pressuring the ball effectively. Encourage players to close down sideways on to allow change of direction more easily. (This is a secondary skill to the main focus, which is first touch into space)

Organisation Of Drill: The drill begins with a pass from Player One to a team mate. This player takes a first touch into space, and lays the ball off to a team mate. Constant movements (unlimited for Player One) develop the concept of moving into space, while having some spare grids allows an 'easy pass' to get the possession going once more, rather like a pass back to a central defender or keeper in a match.

Run the drill for two to three minutes, then swap the attacking and defensive teams over, changing the person acting as Player One.

Development: The white bib is given to Player One, the blue bibs to Player Group Two, the orange bib to Player Three and the red bibs to Player Group Four.

The aim of the drill is to keep possession, using the first touch into space to create the space to play a pass under less pressure. Player One starts anywhere outside the 9 x 9 full grid. This player passes into the feet of any team mate. Player One then moves into the full grid, and can move anywhere, into defended and undefended grids, to be available for a pass.

Player Group Two must make themselves available for a pass. They may NOT enter another grid occupied by another attacker, but have some movement between grids. They receive the pass, make a decision as to which of the first touches into space they will use, and then pass to another player, moving themselves after that either within the grid or into an adjacent one. The most effective way of attacking is to move forward at pace, and the touch into space which delivers this best is the one where the ball goes directly forwards from the touch. Coaches should encourage this touch whenever possible, but players must prioritise keeping possession over this. Thus, over time, they develop the understanding of when the best option is to move forward, and when it is safer to move laterally or backwards.

Within the limitations placed on them, all defensive players attempt to win possession. When they succeed, Player One starts the Drill once again with a pass from outside of the 9 x 9 grid.

The best way to run the drill is to run it for about twenty minutes. Every two minutes change Players One and Three, and after five rotations swap the attacking and defending teams.

A part of the success of this drill is that at any stage the team can move for the 'easy' pass, that is, the one into an undefended grid. The player there has time for a good first touch and to restart the attacking movement. This is just as in a game, a lateral or backwards pass is often an easy option to retain possession, although because it allows defences to re-organise it can rarely break through them. When working with younger teams, where the bigger picture might be lost behind the urge to 'win' it may be necessary to impose limits to prevent every pass being one into an unmarked space.

Development: This drill is best developed by reducing the amount of space the players have to use. This means passing has to be sharper, there are fewer 'safe' passing options and so the first touch has to be crisper to allow the next pass to be made avoiding too much pressure, which in turn affects accuracy. Reducing the full grid to one of 2 x 3 10 x 10 meter grids achieves this.

Drill Six - Difficult

Name of Drill: First Touch Into Space To Create Scoring Opportunities.

Objective of Drill: To create the space and time for a killer pass that becomes an assist for a shot in goal.

Space Required: Half pitch.

Number of Players Involved (multiple spaces can be used for larger groups): Thirteen.

Other Resources: Several balls, bibs.

Roles of Players Involved:

- *Team One* – Attackers.
- *Team Two* – Defenders.
- *Player Three* – Goalkeeper.

Actions of Players Involved:

- *Team One* – Attempt to create goal scoring opportunities.
- *Team Two* – Attempt to prevent goal scoring opportunities.
- *Player Three* – Acts as a goalkeeper.

Key Skills Of Players Involved: These are as in Drill Five. Players use their first touch into space, their decision making, their communication and their movement to either create, or defend against, a shot on goal.

Organisation Of Drill: This is a simple drill to organise. Using half the pitch, the group are divided into two teams plus a goalkeeper. One area is designated for attackers only, so that there is always an easy pass to rebuild an attack, or switch play. This could be the other half of the pitch or, to create more pressure, the D of the centre circle. Added difficulty can be created by allowing one defender to enter this zone.

The aim is to create space with the first touch to enable a killer pass to be delivered. Teams need to be taught the value of patience, and the importance of keeping possession to do this.

Run the drill for ten minutes, then swap the teams over. With younger players, competition can be created by awarding points for certain achievements. For example, one point for a shot, three points for a shot inside the penalty area (harder to create), five points for a shot on target and ten for a goal.

Development: Time pressure can be added to speed play up. An additional attacker can be added to create a 'spare man'.

Drill Seven - Moderate

Name of Drill: First Touch Into Space For A Shot.

Objective of Drill: To develop a first touch which creates a chance for a clean shot with the second.

Space Required: 30 x 20 meters with a goal. This drill works well using half a pitch.

Number of Players Involved (multiple spaces can be used for larger groups): Up to ten, but can be practised with just three.

Other Resources: 4 x balls.

Roles of Players Involved:

- *Player One* – Feeder.
- *Player Group Two* – Four strikers, spread across the pitch.
- *Player Group Three* – A defender for each striker.
- *Player Four* – A goalkeeper.

Actions of Players Involved:

- *Player One* – Feeds a pass for the striker to run onto.
- *Player Group Two* – From their starting positions, they move onto the pass, take a good touch into space and either shoot or dribble past the keeper, and score.
- *Player Group Three* – Starting from the limitation point imposed on them, they seek to apply pressure on the strikers.
- *Player Four* – The goalkeeper uses positioning and goalkeeping skills to try to prevent the opponents from scoring.

Key Skills Of Players Involved:

- *Player One* – Must weigh the pass so that the striker can run onto the ball. This is a particularly important job in this drill.

- *Player Group Two* – Strikers receive the pass at pass, adjusting their feet so that their first touch creates the opportunity for a shot at goal with their next touch. This means the first touch takes the ball:
  - *Along the ground.*
  - *Approximately two meters in front of them.*
  - *Slightly to the side, so that the shooting foot can strike without breaking stride.*
  - *To a position to give themselves enough time to set themselves, i.e. get their balance right for the shot.*
  - *In a way to ensure that their arms and head are in the correct positions to shoot under control. Arms out for balance and to protect from defenders, head over the ball.*
  - *Into a position (i.e. around two meters to the front and slightly to the side of them) which allows a smooth strike with the foot, usually striking the ball with:*
    - The laces for power.
    - The outside of the boot to induce spin.
    - The instep to provide curve, allowing the body to open up and the ball to curve into the far corner.
    - The inside of the toes for a disguised chip.
- *Player Group Three* – Attempts to prevent the shot within the role they are given.
- *Player Four* – The goalkeeper uses positioning and goalkeeping ability to save the shot.

Organisation Of Drill: Depending on the ability levels of the players, there are several stages to the organisation of the drill.

Firstly, attacking players need to identify the *best* options for a strike at goal from their position. Broadly speaking, for a right footed player:

- From wide on the right, either drive a pass across the goal, or put in a cross for a header. If shooting, it is likely to be with the outside of the boot to bring the ball back into the far corner. This is a difficult skill. An alternative might be to drive the ball hard with the laces to the near post in an attempt to beat the goalkeeper with power.
- From centre, to centre right: This is the position where, for the right footer, most options exist. The first touch into space should allow the player to: chip over the goalkeeper, dummy the goalkeeper and beat them with a dribble, 'pass' the ball into the goal with their instep, drive a shot with the laces.
- The centre left, mostly players will open their bodies so that they are chest on to the goal, lean very slightly away from the ball (not too much, or it will soar over the bar) and strike firmly towards the outside of the far post with their instep. The ball should then travel wide of the goalkeeper, but come back and end up inside the far post.

- The wide left, which is the hardest position from which to score for a right footed player. The first touch here will usually be lateral, taking the ball towards the corner of the penalty area. The angle that the player then runs onto the ball allows a powerful strike with the laces towards the outside of the far post which should curl the ball back and into the far corner of the goal. When they come off, these can be spectacular goals.

While the players practice these various finishes, they can do so without defenders. As defenders are gradually increased, they can go through the following stages:

- Stationary, just being a presence beyond which the first touch can take the ball (statues or cones can be used as defenders in this case).
- Chasing back. Here the defender begins between 5 and 10 meters behind the striker, meaning that they have plenty of time to get in their shot provided the first touch is good.
- Full Defending. Gradually defenders can start from closer to the striker until they are marking them properly. In this situation, there will be many less successful opportunities for shooting, so this aspect of the drill should be used sparingly.

The drill works with each attacking player having five shots in each position, and then the teams can swap.

Development: A good development for the drill is to turn it into a team game. The principle works as before. Player One, the feeder, starts with a pass, but it can be to any player. That player then decides whether to shoot after their first touch, or lay off a pass to one of their team mates, who have moved into good goalscoring positions from their own starting points, which are as in the Drill above.

The number of defenders can be gradually introduced until it is 4 v 4.

Drill Seven - Easy

Name of Drill: First Touch and Shot from a Short Pass.

Objective of Drill: To take a good first touch from a short pass leading to a shot.

Space Required: Penalty area and goal.

Number of Players Involved (multiple spaces can be used for larger groups): Three to ten.

Other Resources: Several balls.

Roles of Players Involved:

- *Player One* – The feeder lays a short, 5 meter pass, laterally or slightly backwards to the on – running striker.
- *Player Group Two* – These are the strikers, they are seeking to take a touch and then shoot.
- *Player Three* - Goalkeeper
- *Player Four* – There is not a need for defenders in this drill since, although they would be present in a match, the aim is to develop the skills for the first touch and shot.

Actions of Players Involved:

- *Player One* – To give a short pass.
- *Player Two* – To take a good first touch and shoot.
- *Player Three* – To save the shot.

Key Skills Of Players Involved:

- *Player Group Two* – Firstly to take a good first touch while running. Since the aim will be to not break stride, the touch will be with the outside of the shooting foot if taking the ball back in the direction it is coming from, the instep if taking it further across the goal. The ball should be knocked one to one and a half meters in front of them by the striker, at an angle of around 45 degree. The shot should be across the goal. Since this option would be taken when under pressure, shots on either side should go for power, and therefore be struck with the laces, head over the ball and arms out for balance and protection.

Organisation Of Drill: For a right footed player. Players line up centrally, about 25 meters from the goal. The player about to shoot begins their run. The feeder stands on the edge of the area to the right of the runner and hits a pass across laterally or slightly backwards. The player takes a touch without breaking stride, using the outside of their foot and back towards the direction from which the ball came. They shoot, using the laces, with their next touch.

Next, the feeder stands to the left of the on running strikers. This time the strikers slow slightly as they are about to receive the ball, they let it run across their bodies and direct it approximately one meter forward and sideways in the direction the ball is already traveling in, directing the touch at about 45 degrees. The striker shifts their weight and moves onto the ball, striking it for power.

Development: A static defence can be provided, around which the striker moves the ball with their first touch.

Movement Without The Ball

As we stressed at the beginning of this book, soccer is a simple game. Score more times than your opponent and you win. Of courses, scoring those goals – and preventing the other side from bursting your own net with shots of their own – is often easier said than done.

We looked in the last chapter at how possession of the ball can be used effectively to create goal scoring opportunities. In this one, and the next, we will concentrate on what players can do when they do not have the ball to increase their sides chances of securing victory.

Offensively, movement off the ball seeks to achieve one of two goals:

- To create space for the players off the ball. So, for example, a blindside run (running behind the back of an opponent, which is sometimes known as 'running off' the opponent) can create the angle for a decisive pass, and the space to do something constructive with that pass when it is received.
- To create space for the player on the ball, and other team mates. For example, if Player A is dribbling hard at a defence, and Player B is

seeking to get into a position to receive a pass, when Player C makes a movement without the ball, he could take a defender away as this player tries to cover that run. This, in turn, creates more space for players A and B.

Defensively, movement off the ball is also very important. There are fundamentally four aspects to defending. The first is to pressure the ball and make tackles. The other three, however, movements away from the ball.

- Tracking and covering space. So, when a team mate moves to pressure the ball, or mark a run the space left behind needs to be filled.
- When an opponent makes a run, that run needs to be tracked.
- The third aspect of defensive movement off the ball is the one which most closely fits our definition of soccer intelligence. This is the ability to predict or anticipate where the ball, or runs off the ball, will end up.

We talked about Franz Beckenbauer and Bobby Moore at the beginning of the book, marking them out as two of the most intelligent defensive players of all time. What these players did so remarkably well was to anticipate where the ball would end up. Therefore, they always seemed to be in the right place at the right time. And so, their job was easier.

Offensive movement off the ball is dramatic when it leads to results. The pass hit into the runner's path will cut through the defence, and create shooting or assist opportunities. Watching this movement is aesthetically pleasing. It is the stuff of the $100 million dollar players. It is what the crowd pays its money to watch.

Defensive cover off the ball is less spectacular, it doesn't stick as much in the mind. But at the end of the game, when your side has won 2-0, and the opponent's best player has had a quiet game, it is probably because a defensive player has anticipated, time and again, the movement and passing of their opponents.

Many fine teams are superb with the ball, and their players run off it into space to spectacular effect. These are the teams the neutral fans want to see – the likes of Arsenal, Napoli and Spurs of recent years. But the sides that win championships, they are the ones that also have the defensive intelligence.

France won the recent World Cup, one which many pundits described as one of the most exciting ever. But for all of the attacking thrill of MBappe and Pogba, it was the intelligent running of Olivier Giroud up front, the defensive midfield cover of Ngolo Kante and the teamwork and reading of the game of Umtiti and Varane at the back that sealed their status as best in the world.

A Short message from the Author:

Hey, are you enjoying the book? I'd love to hear your thoughts!

Many readers do not know how hard reviews are to come by, and how much they help an author.

I would be incredibly thankful if you could take just 60 seconds to write a brief review on Amazon, even if it's just a few sentences!

Please head to the product page, and leave a review as shown below.

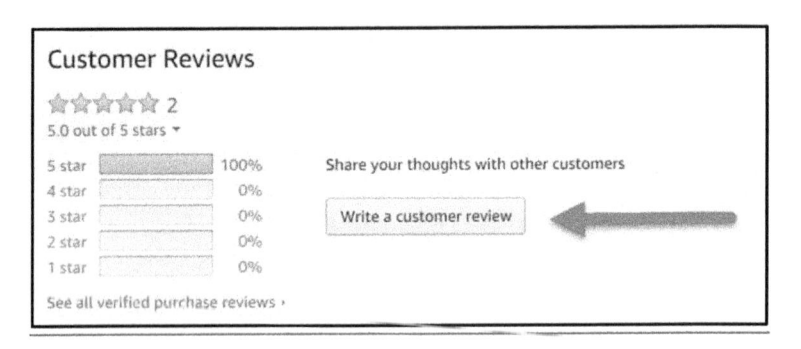

Thank you for taking the time to share your thoughts!

Your review will genuinely make a difference for me and help gain exposure for my work.

Drills To Improve Movement Without The Ball

Drill Eight - Easy

Name of Drill: Squares and Triangles.

Objective of Drill: To encourage players to get into position to receive a key pass.

Space Required: One large grid, minimum 15 x 15 meters (the larger the grid, the easier the exercise becomes). In the middle of the grid, one equilateral triangle with sides of 4 meters, marked out with a cone in each corner. The aim is to pass the ball through the triangle and have it collected and controlled on the other side.

Number of Players Involved (multiple spaces can be used for larger groups): Five.

Other Resources: 1 x ball.

Roles of Players Involved:

- *Player Group One* – These are the attacking players.
- *Player Two* – This is the one defender.

Actions of Players Involved:

- *Player Group One* – To pass and move to create space for a pass to be made through the triangle and received on the other side. Attacking players are not allowed into the triangle, and can pass around the triangle (within the grid) to create a good position for the key pass (i.e., the one that passes through the triangle.)
- *Player Two* – Tried to intercept the pass. He or she is not allowed into the triangle.

Key Skills Of Players Involved:

- *Player Group One* – The main skill being tested is movement to create an angle for a pass. The players will be aiming to read the game so that they can the key pass coming two or three passes down the line. There are secondary skills being developed. These include communication, taking the first touch into space in order to be able to move the ball quickly and accurately. Finally, players will be developing their ability to deliver short, precise and fast passes, sometimes on their first touch, sometimes on the second.

- *Player Two* – If the drill works well, Player Two should not be able to get too near the ball. However, this player is developing anticipation skills, and also physical fitness as they will be moving rapidly and constantly.

Organisation Of Drill: The four attacking players (Player Group One) use quick, short passes to create the space for the key pass. When the opportunity arises, the ball is passed through the triangle to 'score' with the key pass. However, the ball must be received cleanly on the other side of the triangle. The coach should be constantly encouraging intelligent movement, shouting out for players to think two or three passes ahead. The coach should stop the drill regularly to demonstrate how movement could be improved by players interpreting where their team mates will pass.

Encourage attackers to give themselves space away from the triangle to both widen the angles of the passes they can receive, and to give them more options with their first touch into space after receiving the key pass.

Change the defender after each interception, or every two minutes.

Development: The drill can be made more challenging by both adding a second defender, or making the central triangle smaller, say to 3 x 3 x 3 meters.

Drill Nine - Difficult

Name of Drill: Blindside Runs.

Objective of Drill: To encourage players to make blindside runs into space.

Space Required: 20 x 20 meter grid.

Number of Players Involved (multiple spaces can be used for larger groups): Four.

Other Resources: 1 x ball.

Roles of Players Involved: At various times, each player passes, makes a blind side run and receives the pass. It is a very fluid drill.

- *Player One* – Begins in the middle of the left hand line of the grid.
- *Player Two* - Begins ten meters behind Player One, in the bottom corner of the grid.
- *Player Three* – Begins ten meters in front of Player One in the top corner of the grid.
- *Player Four* – Begins opposite Player One on the middle of the right hand line of the grid

Actions of Players Involved:

- *Player One* – Passes to Player Three, then makes a blindside run beyond Player Three. He continues his run and will receive a pass, when approximately half way along the top line of the grid. This pass will be from Player Two. Player One then passes to Player Four, and continues his run until he is now in the top corner of the left hand line of the grid. He is then ready for the drill to be played back from the other side.
- *Player Two* – As Player One makes his first pass, Player Two moves towards the centre of the grid. He receives a short pass there (two meters maximum) from Player Three. Player Two then plays a first time pass into the run of Player One (see above). Player Two

finally moves to position from which Player One began, ready for the drill to be played out from the other side.

- *Player Three* – Player Three receives the pass from Player One then dribbles the ball towards the centre of the grid, while Player One makes his blindside run behind him. Near the centre of the grid, Player Three plays a short pass to the on running Player Two, Player Three then heads into the bottom corner of the left hand line of the grid ready for the drill to be repeated the other way.
- *Player Four* – Player Four receives the final pass of the grid from Player One. She then waits for everybody to get into position, and begins the drill from her side. She repeats the actions of Player One.

Key Skills Of Players Involved: Through the drill, each player will take on each role. The key skills identified below are for the FIRST rotation of the drill.

- *Player One* – This player must:
  o Pass accurately and firmly along the ground, using the instep.
  o Make a blindside run behind his team mate (Player Three), then change the angle of the run by 90 degrees when he reaches the corner of the grid.
  o Makes a first time pass with control and accuracy, using the instep and ensuring that his head is over the ball to keep it on the grass.

- *Player Two* – This player will:
  - Hit a first time pass with accuracy towards a moving team mate. He will play it in front of his team mate so that they can run onto the ball, again keeping head over the ball and striking firmly with the instep to ensure the pass remains low and accurate.
  - Continue a run off the ball.
- *Player Three* – This player will practise the following skills:
  - Receiving a pass with a first touch that knocks it into space allowing him to drive forward.
  - Play a short, controlled pass with the instep while dribbling.
  - Continue a run off the ball.
- *Player Four* – This player receives a pass and controls it with a lateral first touch into space so that he or she can pass to restart the drill.

Organisation Of Drill: This is an excellent drill in many ways. It is fast and fluid. It practises many different skills that are the key to intelligent soccer: first touch into space; passing into space for an on-running player; running off the ball. It also works in a way that allows these skills to be worked on by all players. However, it is complicated. By working through the steps below with the four players (or using a group to demonstrate to the rest of the team) the drill can be understood in a couple of minutes, and then used as a warm up, or warm down, at future sessions.

1. Position players in their starting positions, the ball with Player One.

2. Show each players role individually with you, as coach, performing the roles of other players. So, stand next to Player Three, receive the pass from Player One and dribble towards the middle.

3. Once Players One and Three understand their role, get them to do it while you act as Player Two.

4. And so on, acting as Player Four.

5. Once the demonstration group have the idea, run through it twice (i.e. starting from the right hand line of the grid, then the left hand side.) They are now demonstrating the drill to the remainder of the squad.

6. Coaching points through the actual drill should initially be to make sure all participants have understood their role. Then, focus on the key skill each player needs in the particular run through they are doing.

Development: Pace can be injected by making all passes one touch, in which case Player Three passes, rather than dribbles. Player Two and One need to get into position more quickly to receive their pass.

A goal can be placed 10 meters behind Player Four. This player now turns and shoots on receipt of the pass. OR Players One and Three continue their run beyond the left hand line of the grid. Player Four passes to one of these, who shoot on goal.

Drill Ten – Moderate

Name of Drill: Give and Go.

Objective of Drill: To encourage movement of players when not in possession of the ball. To encourage blind side running.

Space Required: 3 x 10 meter grids, or use lines already marked on a pitch, such as the long lines on the penalty areas, from half way line to the corners, across the half way line.

Number of Players Involved (multiple spaces can be used for larger groups): Three per group.

Other Resources: 1 x ball per group.

Roles of Players Involved:

- *Player One* – Pass and move, receiving the return pass with a first touch into space.
- *Players Two and Three-* Pass and move as above, but movement should be on blindside.

Actions of Players Involved:

- *Player One* - Starts 5 to 10 meters (depending on ability) to the side of the other players, and five meters back from Player Two. Passes and moves to receive a square pass back from Player Two. Player One takes a first touch into space and passes to Player Three. He receives the return as before. By then, Player Two has moved on to receive the next pass, and so on.
- *Player Two* – Starts on the grid line, or touch line, 5 meters up the pitch from Player One. She receives the pass, takes a touch, shifting the ball into space so that they second touch can be a pass. She passes laterally across to Player One, who is moving forwards. Player Two then runs behind and 5 meters beyond Player Three, ready to receive another pass.

- *Player Three* – Starts on the touchline 5 meters up from Player Two. Then plays the same actions as Player Two, making the same blindside run.

Key Skills Of Players Involved:

- *Player One:*
  o Accurate passing up to 10 meters along the ground. The drill only works if the pass is properly directed and weighted to allow for a two touch return pass.
  o Taking a first touch which moves the ball into space ready for the next pass.
  o Moving forwards onto the ball.
- *Players Two and Three:*
  o Receiving the pass with a good first touch which allows the second touch to be a return pass.
  o Passing with accuracy and good weight into a player running on to the pass.
  o Making a blindside run behind another players, accelerating into the space to be ready for the next pass.

Organisation Of Drill: The drill is very fluid. The players set up as above, and move as instructed above. Player One passes to Player

Two and receives the return pass. He then passes to Player Three and again receives the return. By then Player Two has moved into position beyond Player Three, and the pass is made to them. And so on.

Development: One touch passing makes the Drill more challenging and also quicker. Key skills are for players to watch the pass onto their foot, and return the pass firmly, with head over the ball. Once the ball leaves the floor, the drill becomes difficult to complete.

Drill Eleven - Moderate

Name of Drill: Defensive Movement Off The Ball.

Objective of Drill: To develop reading of the game when not in possession.

Space Required: 6 x 10 x 10 meter grids, in a 3 x 2 arrangement, with a small goal at one end. The game is played using the grids as a long, narrow, strip.

Number of Players Involved (multiple spaces can be used for larger groups): Five.

Other Resources: 1 x balls, bibs for teams.

Roles of Players Involved:

- *Player One* – First Defender.
- *Player Two* – Off the Ball defender.
- *Player Group Three* – Attackers.
- *Player Four* – Goalkeeper.

Actions of Players Involved:

- *Player One* – Presses the man with the ball.
- *Player Two* – Covers his fellow defender.
- *Player Group Three* – Attempt to score.
- *Player Four* – Goalkeeper.

Key Skills Of Players Involved:

- *Player One* – Pressing play, seeking to make a tackle.
  o Communication with team mate.
  o Body in correct position, angled to the attacker, offering the better chance to go past on attacker's weaker side, knees bent, on toes.

- Knowing when to change to be covering defender.

- *Player Two* – Covering play.
  - In line with second striker, but five meters closer to goal than defensive partner – to allow for cover to team mate plus anticipating the pass to the other striker to close down.
  - Communication.
  - Knowing when to become the pressing players (when the ball is passed, or if the striker with the ball gets past the other defender).

- *Player Group Three* – Not the focus of the drill.

- *Player Four* – Not the focus of the drill.

Organisation Of Drill: Goalkeeper begins with the ball. Two defenders begin in the middle set of grids, two attackers in the end set of grids, furthest from the goal.

The goalkeeper kicks the ball out to the strikers. They will then attempt to create the opportunity to score.

Player One (the nearest to the striker with the ball), closes to pressure and harry.

Player Two adopts the cover position, both covering team mate and getting ready to pressure the other striker if the ball is passed to them.

Allow twenty five seconds for the strikers to get in a shot at goal.

Rotate the players.

Development: The drill can grow with 3 v 3 and 4 v 4, using a bigger pitch as the numbers grow.

Drill Twelve - Difficult

Name of Drill: Focus Game (Movement off the ball).

Objective of Drill: For players to develop both offensive and defensive movement off the ball.

Space Required: Small pitch.

Number of Players Involved (multiple spaces can be used for larger groups): Fourteen or Sixteen (seven a side or eight a side).

Other Resources: Several balls and bibs.

Roles of Players Involved:

- *All Players* – Play a normal small sided game.

Actions of Players Involved:

- *All Players* – The focus of the game is twofold:
  o To use effective offensive and defensive movement off the ball.
  o To switch roles at transition.

Key Skills Of Players Involved:

- *All Players* – In the context of a normal game:
  o Make good runs off the ball;
  o Track runs off the ball;
  o Anticipate passes and runs;
  o Communicate.

Organisation Of Drill: This is very much a coach driven drill. Basically, a normal game is played. However, players are told that the focus is on movement off the ball.

The coach must stop the game regularly to point out good movement off the ball, to ask players directly what they are doing at a particular moment in the game, to suggest movements off the ball that could be made. The aim is to bring this aspect of the game to the forefront of the players' thinking.

Development: If players are struggling, especially younger, less experienced teams, the coach can provide set movements. For example, at transition he or she can instruct players to make particular movements. For example, she can say 'When the ball is intercepted centrally in the defensive half, whoever is acting as full back at that time pulls wide and pushes forward.'

Where the drill is working, and players are running off the ball, the coach can increase numbers up to 11 v 11.

Because this type of game is very broken, it is suggested that it is limited to ten minutes. If the facilities allow, video of the game and then analysis with the players can help to reinforce the objectives we are trying to instil into the players.

Choosing Between Passes

It was probably the Total Football team of Ajax, and then the Dutch National team, that planted the seeds. But today's footballers do need to be able to do everything. Striker's need to defend, full backs transform into wingers…

And that means an expectation that every player on the park can pass the ball. Not only with accuracy, but selecting the correct option when passing. We literally mean every player. Including the goalkeeper. Many teams now seek to start by playing from the back. No longer is it enough for the goalkeeper to be able to kick the ball hopefully two thirds of the length of the pitch. Against good teams, if such a kick results in a loss of possession, then the team might not touch the ball for another thirty passes.

So even the goalkeeper must be able to receive a pass, play short and also hit long, often diagonal balls to get play moving further up the pitch. Manchester City, current English Premier League Champions and favourites for the 2018-19 Champions League, saw their manager (Pep Guardiola) discard the England goalkeeper, Joe Hart, because he felt the player's distribution was not good enough. By bringing in the Brazilian, Everson, Guardiola added another dimension to his team, allowing his side to effectively become 11 v 10 when in possession. Other sides are now following suit. Jordan Pickford, in many people's eyes the top performing goalkeeper at the recent World Cup, was selected ahead of two equally talented stoppers because of his ability as a passer.

For all this, it is the great passers, the ones who turn defence into attack, who penetrate the opposition back line with an impossible angle and perfectly weighted delivery, to whom we should aspire.

The David Silva or Mesut Ozil of a team. So what is it that makes a great passer of the ball?

Technical Ability;

Excellent First Touch;

Good communication;

Strength of Character;

And, of course, soccer intelligence. Perhaps, in this scenario, we might call it vision.

But selecting the right pass is more than just instinct. As with all other aspects of soccer, practice and applying theory can result in the best pass.

A great pass only works if the recipient gets on the end of it. So the following tips on the attributes above can help to improve the effectiveness of passing.

Technical Ability

Although this book is not designed to deal with this aspect of a player's performance, the best passers are comfortable with both feet. They can control the ball into space with their first touch, giving them time and deliver passes short, long, with the instep and outside of the foot. In other words, the complete range.

Good Communication

They let their team mates know their intention, and respond quickly to the guidance of their fellow players. Sometimes, commentators talk of telepathic communication between, say, a Number 10 and a centre forward. But it is not telepathy; it is practice and time playing together, good communication, a first touch which gives time for the decisive pass to follow and the technical ability to weight the pass as required. All of these abilities can be acquired through practice.

Strength of Character

Passers need to be brave. Sensible as well, but the best passers take risks. The short, lateral or backwards pass will retain possession, which is important, but at some stage (ideally, straight away during the transition phase as possession changes between teams) the killer pass needs to be delivered.

If every such pass came off, then both teams would score into double figures regularly. So there has to be a preparedness to risk the approbation of team mates and the crowd because not every pass will work, and sometimes it would have been a better option to play safe.

But, the best passers are match winners, and by definition, match winners are risk takers.

Drills To Improve Intelligent Passing

The drills we will consider in this section are focussed on the selection of passes, rather than the technical skills of making a pass.

Drill Thirteen- Moderate

Name of Drill: Check Back and Pass.

Objective of Drill: To create the opportunity for a decisive pass by drawing space away from a defence.

Space Required: Half a pitch. Two cones are placed 3 meters apart, with the widest on the corner of the penalty area. The other is 3 meters in along the edge of the penalty area.

Number of Players Involved (multiple spaces can be used for larger groups): Five.

Other Resources: 1 x balls, 2 x cones.

Roles of Players Involved:

- *Player One* – The Passer.
- *Player Two* – The Striker.
- *Player Three* – The Runner.
- *Player Four* – The Defender.
- *Player Five* – The goalkeeper.

Actions of Players Involved:

- *Player One* – Starts on the edge of the central D, and plays a pass to Player Two. Player One then sets off on a run forward. She receives the return, takes a first touch into space, and passes with the instep at an angle through the two cones, for Player Three to run onto.
- *Player Two* – Starts on the edge of the penalty area D. She comes towards Player One, square on, and lays a first or second time pass back to Player One. She then peels off to the opposite side of the penalty area as Player Three.
- *Player Three* – Starts on the touchline level with Player One. Makes a run outside of the cone. Ends with a shot or cross when she receives the ball.
- *Player Four* – Provides pressure on Player Two, and tries to track their run.

- *Player Five* – Goalkeeper.

Key Skills Of Players Involved:

- *Player One* :
  o Firm passing with the instep;
  o Good first touch into space;
  o Good weight of final pass.
- *Player Two* – Must lay off the ball into feet with accuracy and control.
- *Player Three* – Times their run to get onto the end of the through pass. Shoots with power, or crosses with accuracy, away from the keeper.
- *Players Four and Five* – Not relevant for this drill.

Organisation Of Drill: Player One starts with the ball and lays it into Player Two. Player One receives a return pass and then lays a pass at an angle for the on running Player Three, who tries to score either with a shot, or a cross to Player Two.

Development: The drill begins with instep passing, which is the easiest to weight and maintain accuracy. The drill can be developed by getting Player One to try different kinds of passes, including chips for the winger to run on to, or passes with the outside of the foot.

Drill Fourteen - Moderate

Name of Drill: Reverse Pass.

Objective of Drill: To create space for a team mate with a reverse, or disguised, pass.

Space Required: 3 x 3 10 x 10 meter grids, with cones marking the central grid, one in each corner.

Number of Players Involved (multiple spaces can be used for larger groups): Five.

Other Resources: 1 x ball, 4 x cones (to mark central grid.

Roles of Players Involved:

- *Player Group One* – Passers.
- *Player Two* – Defender.

Actions of Players Involved:

- *Player Group One* – Players begin on one side each of the square. They move along the side aiming to create space and an angle for a pass. The player with the ball aims to pass the ball through the central square for a team mate. To make the drill realistic, and to stop the defender from knowing which pass will be delivered, the pass can be of any kind, although it is the reverse pass we are practising.
- *Player Two* – Is in the middle square, and aims to intercept the pass.

Key Skills Of Players Involved:

- *Player Group One* –
  o The reverse pass. Player dribbles. Player shapes to pass in the direction of travel, using the instep.
  o At the last minute, wraps his foot around the ball to bring it back against the direction of travel.
  o Player disguises the pass by using the eyes to look in the expected travel of the pass.
  o Player drops shoulder over passing foot at the last moment, to prevent the pass being spotted.

- *Player Two* – Not the focus of this drill.

Organisation Of Drill: The is an easy drill to set up, more difficult to execute. The players on the outside of the grid simply pass the ball through the defended middle square, using the reverse pass at times to disguise the pass away from the defender.

The passer should be moving when they deliver the pass.

Development: If players are struggling to perfect the technique, the drill can revert to being without a defender. Making the central grid smaller requires the pass to be sharper and more disguised.

Drill Fifteen - Difficult

Name of Drill: Through Pass on the Turn.

Objective of Drill: To deliver a through pass on the turn to a player making a blind side run.

Space Required: 4 x (10 x 10) meter grids.

Number of Players Involved (multiple spaces can be used for larger groups): Five.

Other Resources: 1 x ball, five cones. Four of the cones are spread at 5 meter intervals on the line marking the third and fourth set of grids. They begin 5 meters in from the touchline of the grids. They represent static defenders. The fifth cone sits one meter forward, in grid row three, and between cones 2 and 3. This represents the player marking Player Two. The goal is beyond the grids.

Roles of Players Involved:

- *Player One* – Feeder.
- *Player Two* – Passer.
- *Player Group Three* – Runners.
- Player Four – Goalkeeper.

Actions of Players Involved:

- *Player One* – Starts at one end and in the centre of the grids. She passes the ball firmly into the feet of player two, then continues a support run.

- *Player Two* - This player starts with their cone/defender goal side and behind them. They move towards the ball on the half turn. They take a first touch with the outside of the boot, creating a turn. They then pass, on the angle onto one of the on-running team mates from Player Group Three.
- *Player Group Three* – Start on the outside corners of the lines between grid rows one and two. They break on the blind side of the static defenders to run onto the through ball, and shoot.
- *Player Four* – Goalkeeper.

Key Skills Of Players Involved:

- *Player One* – Firm and accurate first pass to feet.
- *Player Two* – The main player in the drill.
   o Move towards Player one, weight forward, knees bent and shoulder towards the pass.
   o Take a controlled touch with the outside of the boot into space to allow the turn.
   o Weight the pass between defenders for the on running strikers.
- *Player Group Three:*
   o Time their run to arrive for the pass.
   o Communicate where they want the pass.
   o Finish with a shot.

- *Player Four* – Not the focus of the drill.

Organisation Of Drill: The drill runs as above. Players can rotate after each run through. The challenge is to get the weight of Player Two's pass right, because they will be running on to the pass they give, and therefore might over hit it.

Development: Use real, rather than static, defenders.

Also, Player Two can dribble after the turn and then use the reverse pass to disguise their delivery to the team mate.

Drill Sixteen - Moderate

Name of Drill: Pass In Behind.

Objective of Drill: To pass into space for a striker to spin into.

Space Required: Half pitch with goal, the width of the penalty area.

Number of Players Involved (multiple spaces can be used for larger groups): Four.

Other Resources: 1 x ball.

Roles of Players Involved:

- *Player One* – Passer.
- *Player Two* – Striker.
- *Player Three* – Defender.
- *Player Four* – Goalkeeper.

Actions of Players Involved:

- *Player One* – Starts on the half way line. She then dribbles around 5-10 meters and delivers a pass into space following the instructions from Player Two.
- *Player Two* – Starts on the edge of the D. Moves towards the ball, indicates where they want the pass, spins off and shoots.
- *Player Three* – Defender, tries to stay close to the striker (Player Two).
- *Player Four* – Goalkeeper.

Key Skills Of Players Involved:

- *Player One* – Weighting the pass into space.
- Getting an angle on the pass stops it from running through to the keeper.
- Either the instep or the outside of the foot can be used. A pass with the outside of the boot, and inside the defender, will spin into the path of the on running striker, taking the defender out of the game, but is hard to deliver.
- *Player Two* -
  o Getting body position right to spin off the defender. (See earlier chapter).
  o Communicating to Player One where they want the ball.
  o Accelerating onto the ball and getting the shot away.
- *Player Three and four* – Not the focus of the exercise.

Organisation Of Drill: Player One can run at different speeds and different angles. This creates the opportunity for different types of passes into the space behind the defender. Player Two should practise sometimes turning onto their weaker side, or they are easy to defend against.

Players can rotate after each run through.

Development: Increasing the number of players to three attackers and two defenders (plus a goalkeeper, makes the drill more realistic to the game situation.

Predicting Opponent's Passing

We have talked about some of the great defenders of the game. However, the modern game has adapted from the days of the greats we have discussed.

Nowadays, every player is expected to perform defensive duties, as well as offensive ones. It is through this effective defensive work that players can improve their anticipation of a pass, and increase their ability to intercept.

There are two simple rules to follow. The nearest player should always press the ball, but the rest of the team make a decision. If the ball is under the opposition's control, with time and space with the ball player, then the team drops off. This narrows space in the crucial attacking third of the opponent, meaning that there is a good chance of the attack breaking down, through interception, mis control or tackle, when the ball is played into this area. It also means that there is no space for players to run into behind the defence.

However, if the player in possession is under pressure, and even more so if there are poor passing options on, then defensively the team should press, narrowing space further up the park and meaning that any pass can be predicted (if there is only one player free, then, in all likelihood, that is where the pass will go) and therefore more readily intercepted.

This point was exemplified in the 2018 Champions League Final. As Liverpool pressed the Real midfield, the only option left was a hopeful flighted ball over the top, which the keeper claimed with ease. That he then threw the ball against Karim Benzema, leading to it being deflected into the net (watch the goal if you haven't seen it!) is something for which no coach could plan. Then, later in the game, failure of anybody to pressure led to a cross field ball to Marcello. This then gave the defender room to get in a precise cross and, again as those who have seen it will know, one of the greatest finishes in soccer history followed.

Interestingly, both teams in the World Cup final of 2018, Croatia and France, were so well drilled defensively that all of the six goals were either long shots, one off errors or from set pieces. Get a team defending well and together, and the opposition are left looking for scraps from which to score.

The following drills work on defensive plays, leading to more chance of an interception, or a side winning back possession.

Drills To Improve Passing Interception

Drill Seventeen

Name of Drill: Closing Down from the Front.

Objective of Drill: To force an interception or long, hopeful pass by pressurising from the front.

Space Required: 3 x 2; 10 x 10 meter grids.

Number of Players Involved (multiple spaces can be used for larger groups): Nine.

Other Resources: 1 x ball, bibs to mark out two teams. Four cones, one in each corner of the grid set.

Roles of Players Involved:

- *Player Group One* – Begin with possession.

- *Player Group Two* – Three players to close down.
- *Player Three* – Player to drop off.
- *Player Four* – Feeder.

Actions of Players Involved:

- *Player Group One* – Begin opposite end to the feeder. Start by one of the cones, run together to the opposite cone (by the feeder). They must then try to play out by crossing the other end of the cone set with the ball under control.
- *Player Group Two* – Three players. They begin from the opposite corner to the first group. They run to the opposite cone and then fan out to pressure the players in possession.
- *Player Three* -This player sets off with his team mates, but on arriving on the pitch, drops off to collect the interception pass
- *Player Four* – The feeder plays the first pass to Group One, then drops out of the drill.

Key Skills Of Players Involved:

- *Player Group One* – Not the focus of the drill.
- *Player Group Two* -

- Work collectively to pressure the man on the ball, limiting passing options.
- Communicate to ensure that the 'free' opponent can always be closed quickly.
- Maintain correct, sideways body position to ensure they can turn and react quickly.
- *Player Three* – Drops 10 meters behind the pressing player. Moves across the pitch at around 30 degrees to the ball, to intercept the pass. Becomes the pressing player if the ball is shifted wide, with the opposite side pressing player dropping into this role.
- Therefore the skill is always about reading the game, anticipating, in the light of the positions of the opposition players, and the pressure they are under, where the pass will go.

Organisation Of Drill: The drill starts with both teams running to opposite corners of the pitch so that they have to work to get into position. The coach should encourage communication. The sides change roles when possession changes, a tackle is made or the ball goes out of the playing area.

Development: The game can be extended by the attacking side gaining a couple of defenders, and the defensive group a couple of attackers. Ultimately, the drill can become a match practice.

Drill Eighteen - Difficult

Name of Drill: Acting as the CDM (central defensive midfielder) and Cutting Out Through Balls.

Objective of Drill: To perform the role of a central defensive midfielder effectively.

Space Required: Full Pitch.

Number of Players Involved (multiple spaces can be used for larger groups): 7 v 7 up to 11 v 11.

Other Resources: 1 x ball, bibs to create two teams.

Roles of Players Involved: For this drill, a normal game is played with the coach concentrating on the effectiveness of the CDM players.

- *CDM* – To ensure that attacks do not penetrate through the centre of the pitch.

Actions of Players Involved:

- *CDM* – Covers the central area of the pitch, filling in for centre halves if they get drawn out of position, and tracking runs beyond the ball.

Key Skills Of Players Involved:

- *CDM*
  o Communicating with back four
  o Positional discipline – staying central and behind the rest of the midfield (or ensuring that another player covers if the CDM moves forward.
  o Passing quickly at transition, ideally forwards, to start attacks.
  o Skills and vision of good passing (as per other drills).

Organisation Of Drill: Because the role of the CDM is very fluid, it is best practised in a match situation. While the individual skills – tackling, intercepting, passing, tracking runners, can be worked on in isolation, it is the fluidity of a game situation where the player will improve and learn.

The coach should stop the game, or speak with the CDMs regularly, identifying good and bad play. Video support is useful if it is to hand.

Development: Different formations to include 2 x CDM.

Drill Nineteen - Easy

Name of Drill: Central Defenders – When To Drop Off.

Objective of Drill: To improve decision making for when to drop off, to improve likelihood of intercepting through balls.

Space Required: Half pitch.

Number of Players Involved (multiple spaces can be used for larger groups): Nine.

Other Resources: 6 x balls, two lines of cones, bibs for teams. The cones make two lines running across the pitch. The more advanced one sits two thirds of the way forward between the edge of the penalty area and the half way line. This is the advanced line. (Depending on the speed of defenders, the pace of the opposition etc) this line might be further forward. The second line is the deep line, and runs level with the apex of the D.

Roles of Players Involved:

- *Player Group One* – Back four (or it can be a three or five, depending on the formation).
- *Player Group Two* – Two attackers.
- *Player Three* – Passer.
- *Player Four* – Pressuriser.
- *Player Five* – Goalkeeper.

Actions of Players Involved:

- *Player Group One* – The back division work in unison. The two centre backs should be close, with one slightly deeper. This is the leader of the group. The two full backs in line with the advanced centre back. The back division start on the advanced line of defensive cones.
- *Player Group Two* – Two strikers who come short, spin in behind and generally try to get a shot in on goal.
- *Player Three* – Tries to pass in to feet, beyond the defence and so forth. He can join in the attack once the initial pass is made. Sometimes, this player can dribble at the back four.
- *Player Four* – The pressurising player is sometimes used, sometimes not.
- *Player Five* – Goalkeeper.

Key Skills Of Players Involved:

- *Player Group One –*
  - Communication;
  - Tracking runs;
  - Moving up together if playing offside;
  - Judging when to drop to the deep line.
- *Player Group Two* – These players try to create the opportunity for a shot on goal.
- *Player Three* – The Passer decides when to pass early, short, long and when to dribble. The coach might play this role, as he can then work on identified weaknesses in the defence.
- *Player Four* – The coach will say when he wants pressure to be strong, weak, or non-existent.
- *Player Five* – The goalkeeper is important in this drill. The most relevant skill in this drill is positioning; when to come for the ball, when to drop for a back pass, when to set for a shot etc. Communication is also important.

Organisation Of Drill: Player Three starts with the ball inside the other half. The coach decides whether there will be pressure on the ball and how much. Player Three seeks to dribble or pass to create chances for Player Group Two. Player Group One make the decision whether to push forward – pressure on the ball, increased chance of interception; or drop back to the deep line, to make a pass behind the defence hard (the goalkeeper should clean up any such ball.)

If the ball is played in behind, the defence should turn and drift across towards the ball, keeping their shape. The opposite full back must be aware of any late runners.

Development: Add a CDM and an attacking midfielder to break beyond the strikers. CDM and centre halves work out who will track this player.

Drill Twenty - Difficult

Name of Drill: Defending as a Team.

Objective of Drill: To defend as a team to win possession.

Space Required: Full Pitch.

Number of Players Involved (multiple spaces can be used for larger groups): 11 v 11 (or whatever is the full sides for the age group.)

Other Resources: 8 x balls, coloured cones, bibs to make two teams. The cones are placed around the outside of the pitch so the coach can direct players to the correct position, e.g. 'Defence in line with the red cone.'

Organisation Of Drill: The drill is designed to develop defensive skills. Plays begin with a dead ball. This can be with any of the back five, or CDM including the keeper. The team make the decision as where to press and when to drop. From each position, and from the level of pressure the coach decides upon, the team sets up its formation. For example, long kick from the keepers' hands – defensive line advanced by drop back when ball is kicked, unless you are the player attacking the ball. CDM to get in front of the attacker to whom the ball is aimed.

Short play out from the back: front players pressure. Defensive line advanced. Midfield covers space.

Opponents on the break through midfield: CDM attempts to cover. Defence drops (as there is time on the ball.) Players watch for breaks on the blind side. Other players who were caught in attack try to make their way back for the next phase.

The coach sets up these situations, and then plays them, analysing the plays that ensue.

Development: The game is artificial, in that the coach decides the starting point, and just that phase of the game is played out, before another begins. The development is to try the who team defence in a real match situation. This brings in the ability to turn defence into attack during the transition phase.

Bonus – The Best Drill Of All Time

Drill Twenty-One – Difficult: The Ultimate Drill For All Soccer Intelligence Skills

Name of Drill: Triple Zones.

Objective of Drill: To keep possession by employing excellent first touch into space plus short and long passing. Also to intercept possession by pressuring and anticipating passes.

Space Required: Three rectangular grids, 25 meters wide by 10 meters deep. The drill works well with dividing half a pitch into three equal 'strips'. Each rectangular grid is called a zone, with zones 1 and 3 at the ends and zone 2 in the middle.

Number of Players Involved (multiple spaces can be used for larger groups): Fifteen to Eighteen.

Other Resources: 1 x ball; 3 x sets of bibs, one set for each team of five.

Roles of Players Involved:

- *Player Group One* – To keep possession, and send it along to the temporary team mates in zone three.
- *Player Group Two* – To pressure and intercept the ball as it is passed through their zone 2.
- *Player Group Three* – To receive passes with good control and first touch into space from their temporary team mates in zone 1.

Actions of Players Involved:

- *Player Group One* – Start with the ball. Pass it within the group, bypassing the pressuring player from Player Group Two, until the angle and opportunity is on for a good pass into zone 3, without interception in group 2.
- *Player Group Two* – To position themselves ready to anticipate passes between the two end groups in zones 1 and 3. One player from Player Group Two is allowed into the grid where the ball is (but not the other grid, until the ball reaches there). That player can change at any

time, but there can never be more than one player in the end grid where the ball is being passed.)

- *Player Group Three* – Receive the long pass from zone 1, using good first touch into space. Then, to create the angle to pass the ball back into zone 1.

Key Skills Of Players Involved:

- *Player Group One and Three:*
  o Good first touch into space to ensure possession is retained and a simple pass to a player in a better position to make a long pass can be given. Note, some passes received will be short, some long.
  o Create angles for both long and short passes.
  o Deliver passes, along the ground for short ones, and while long passes can be in the air if necessary, being aware that passing in this way increases the risk of possession being lost.
  o Communicate to create the opportunity for the decisive long pass.
  o Anticipating the risk of loss of possession, and then getting closer to the player receiving the ball to make their pass easier.

- *Player Group Two:*
  o Pressuring:

- *Communication so that the best player can be sent into pressure the ball.*
- *Judgement as to when that player should be swapped to one in a better position.*
- *Teamwork as the space vacated by the player pressuring the ball is vacated.*
- *Anticipation of where passes will occur so that they can be intercepted.*
  - *Intercepting the Pass.*
- *Anticipation of where the long pass might be made.*
- *Closing angles to make the long pass difficult (i.e. shifting as a team in the direction of the ball to close down the space for a long pass, making the team in the end zone perhaps play it back the other way in their grid.)*

Organisation Of Drill: This is an excellent drill which, once learned, can be used to really develop teamwork and communication, as well as spatial awareness and soccer intelligence.

The ball begins in zone one with Player Group One. One player from Player Group Two, based in zone two, can enter zone one to try to win the ball, or pressure the group into making a bad pass which can be intercepted. (Note: younger teams might often try to pre-determine the roles of players, for example: 'I'll make the long pass' or 'I'll go to challenge for the ball.' The coach needs to encourage them to adapt to the circumstances of the drill, not decide in advance who will perform which roles.

Player Group One try to work as a team to create the angle to pass the ball through or over zone two and into zone three. If they succeed, they score a point.

Player Group Three then try to get the ball under control and pass it back to Player Group One. If they do so, they score a point, although a player from Player Group Two will move into their zone to try to win the ball. (Note: while a high pass is less likely to be intercepted, controlling the receipt of that long pass is harder. This means that the ball might bounce out of the grid, or the pressurising player can make a tackle and put the ball out of the grid. Players should be encouraged to develop the long term skill of passing on the ground, resorting to the lifted pass only if they must.)

If the ball leaves the grid, or is intercepted by Player Group Two in zone 2, then the last team to play the ball swap with Player Group Two, move to zone 2 and become the defenders.

Playing the game with the first of the three teams to score twenty points works well, taking about 10 minutes usually.

Development: Making the central grid smaller makes the drill easier, but enlarging it makes the drill tougher.

Conclusion

There is no doubt that all the skill in the world, all the pace, all the strength can be nullified by soccer intelligence in defense and enhanced with intelligent moves among the front players.

And that intelligence does not have to be innate. By following the drills, we have covered in this book, and developing them into practices that suit your own team's situations, we can instill soccer intelligence into any player.

We ask that coaches simply request this from their teams:

- Practise techniques so that we can utilize our intelligence to the best effect. It is no good seeing a pass if you cannot deliver it.
- Ensure physical fitness. When the body is tired, then the brain becomes less efficient.
- Communicate. It is no good having a brilliant move in mind if nobody else knows what is in our head.

- Keep it simple. In possession, create space, out of possession, close it down.

The best teams and the best players are full of soccer intelligence, and there is nothing wrong with learning from the best.

The end… almost!

Reviews are not easy to come by.

As an independent author with a tiny marketing budget, I rely on readers, like you, to leave a short review on Amazon.

Even if it's just a sentence or two!

So if you enjoyed the book, please head to the product page, and leave a review as shown below.

I am very appreciative for your review as it truly makes a difference.

Thank you from the bottom of my heart for purchasing this book and reading it to the end.